Activate!
15 Keys To Activating Your Ear To Hear The Voice Of God

By

Kajsa Cole

Copyright © 2025 Kajsa Cole

All rights reserved. No part of this publication may be reproduced, distributed, or transmitted in any form or by any means without the prior written permission of the author.

ISBN:

Dedication

To my beloved family, thank you for being the constant heartbeat behind everything I do.

To **my husband, Scotty,** you are my covering, my greatest encourager, and my anchor in both life and ministry. Your unwavering love, quiet strength, and sacrificial leadership have allowed me to flourish in my purpose. Thank you for holding me up in moments when I didn't feel strong and for consistently reminding me of who I am in God. I am better, stronger, and more grounded because of you.

To **my daughter, Zion,** you are my beautiful reflection and a radiant light in this world. Watching you grow into a powerful young woman of God has been one of the greatest joys of my life. Your fire, faith, and boldness inspire me daily.

To **my son, Jonathan**, you are my joy and my reminder of God's promise. Your curiosity, tenderness, and growing faith warm my heart and give me hope for the future.

To **my mother, Brenda Flanders,** thank you for planting seeds of faith in me early. Your strength, prayers, and nurturing heart helped shape the foundation of the woman I've become. I honor you deeply.

To **my sisters, Tajsa, Taneisha, and Brenna,** thank you for being my built-in tribe. You've supported me through every season with love, laughter, and loyalty. Each of you carries a piece of my heart, and I'm grateful to walk this life with you.

To **my ministry sisters**, you've poured with me, prayed with me, fasted, labored, laughed, cried, and carried the weight of the Gospel beside me. Thank you for your accountability, your love, and your sisterhood in the trenches of ministry. Our bond is eternal. You've helped sharpen me, and I'm better because of your presence in my life.

To **my pastor, Pastor Jennifer** Biard of Jackson Revival Center Church (JRC), thank you for your leadership, love, and example. Your wisdom, guidance, and anointed teaching have helped shape my spiritual walk. I am grateful for your covering and for the freedom to grow under your pastoral care. Your voice of truth and grace has been both an anchor and fuel for my journey.

And to **my spiritual mother and lifelong friend, Tonyia "Peaches" Fairley Benton**, this work is especially dedicated to you. You were my Naomi—my wise counselor, my cheerleader, my quiet intercessor, and my mirror of grace. You saw me before I saw myself, called out the anointing in me, and challenged me to hear God for myself when it wasn't easy.

Your passing in 2021 left a deep void, but your voice still echoes in my spirit. You were my midwife in the spirit, guiding me through some of my most defining moments. You taught me that hearing God independently is the greatest asset a believer can have. You modeled the urgency of intimacy with the Father, and now I carry that message in everything I do.

Your mantle has fallen, and I feel its weight with reverence. Your legacy lives on through every word I write, every message I preach, and every soul I touch. I miss you deeply, but I will honor you faithfully. Thank you for making room for me to grow, to lead, and to become. I will carry your name and your spirit with honor for the rest of my life.

With all my love,

Kajsa

Acknowledgments

To my beloved sisters in the gospel—your prayers, encouragement, and unwavering commitment to the work of the Kingdom have been a constant source of strength. Thank you for standing beside me as faithful co-laborers, lifting each other up in love, truth, and purpose. Whether in moments of celebration or seasons of spiritual warfare, your presence has been both a shield and a song. This journey would not be as rich without your voices, your anointing, and your yes to God. I honor each of you for the powerful roles you play in advancing His glory.

Contents

Hearing and Understanding the Voice of God: A Biblical Perspective 1
   Introduction 1
   The Nature of God's Voice 1
      1. God's Voice in Creation 1
      2. The Still Small Voice 2
      3. The Voice of the Prophets 2
   Understanding God's Voice 2
      4. The Role of the Holy Spirit 2
      5. Scripture as God's Voice 3
      6. Prayer and Meditation 3
   Responding to God's Voice 3
      7. Obedience and Action 3
      8. Discernment and Testing 4
      9. Community and Accountability 4
   Key 1: Prayer 5
      Turn the Key Exercise 6
      Simple Prayer 6
   Key 2: Posture – The Position of Alignment 7
      Definition & Importance 7
      Spiritual Postures That Invite God's Presence 7
      Signs of a Wrong Posture 8
      Turn the Key: A Posture Check 9
      Prayer for Posture Alignment 9

Key 3: Pursuit – The Passionate Chase after God 10
- Definition & Importance 10
- Pursuit Is a Requirement, Not an Option 10
- Are You a Seeker? 11
- What Can Hinder Your Pursuit? 12
- Turn the Key: Rekindle Your Pursuit 12
- Prayer for a Renewed Pursuit 13

Key 4: Purge – A Cleansing for Clarity 14
- Definition & Importance 14
- Why Do We Need to Be Purged? 14
- The Ear Gate: Guarding Your Spiritual Intake 15
- The Benefits of Purging 16
- Turn the Key: A Self-Purging Inventory 16
- Prayer for Purging & Cleansing 17

Key 5: Pattern – Aligning Your Life for Growth 18
- Definition & Importance 18
- The Power of Patterns 18
- Turn the Key: Align Your Patterns 19
- Prayer for Realignment 19

Key 6: Pain – The Teacher of Transformation 20
- Definition & Importance 20
- Pain Produces Purpose 20
- Turn the Key: Learn from Your Pain 21
- Prayer for Strength in Pain 21

Key 7: Passion – Rekindling Your Fire for God 22

  Definition & Importance 22

  What Passion for God Looks Like 22

  Turn the Key: Reignite Your Passion 22

  Prayer for Renewed Passion 23

Key 8: Perception – Seeing as God Sees 24

  Teaching 24

  Realigning Our Perception with God's Vision 25

  Turn the Key – Practical Exercise 26

  Simple Prayer 27

Key 9: Persistence – Pressing In Until You Hear God 28

  Teaching 28

  Turn the Key – Practical Exercise 31

  Simple Prayer 31

Key 10: Practice – Walking in Daily Obedience 32

  Teaching 32

  How to Practice Hearing and Obeying the Holy Spirit 33

  Turn the Key – Practical Exercise 34

  Simple Prayer 34

Key 11: Pace – Walking in Step with God's Timing 36

  Teaching 36

The Dangers of Rushing Through Life 36

  God is Not Bound by Time 37

  Turn the Key – Practical Exercise 38

  Simple Prayer 38

Key 12: Praise – Unlocking the Power of Worship 40

Definition & Importance 40
Why Praise is Powerful 40
Turn the Key: Activate Your Praise 41
Prayer for a Life of Praise 41

Key 13: Pivoting – Embracing God's Divine Redirection 42
Definition & Importance 42
When Does God Call Us to Pivot? 42
Turn the Key: Trust the Pivot 43
Prayer for Trust in God's Direction 43

Key 14: Proclaiming – Declaring the Word with Boldness 44
Definition & Importance 44
Why Proclaiming God's Word Is Essential 44
Turn the Key: Speak Life 45
Prayer for Bold Proclamation 45

Key 15: Pleasing God – Living for an Audience of One 46
Definition & Importance 46
What Pleases God? 46
Turn the Key: Live for God's Approval 46
Prayer for a Life that Pleases God 47

Conclusion: Unlocking a Life of Hearing God 48
The Responsibility of Hearing 48
Staying in Position to Hear 49
Your Next Step 49
Final Prayer 50
Biblical Meditations to Help Hear from God 51

1. Seeking God's Voice 51
2. Removing Spiritual Blockages 51
3. Trusting God's Timing 52
4. Aligning Your Heart with God's Will 52
5. The Power of God's Word 53
6. Asking and Expecting to Hear from God 54
7. Walking in Obedience to What You Hear 54
Final Thought: Position Yourself to Hear 55

Hearing and Understanding the Voice of God: A Biblical Perspective

Introduction

From Genesis to Revelation, Scripture unfolds a rich and multifaceted dialogue between God and humanity. The voice of God is not merely an abstract concept but a dynamic reality that has shaped the course of history, transformed lives, and revealed the depths of divine wisdom. As believers, cultivating the ability to hear and discern God's voice is not only a spiritual privilege but a necessity for walking in alignment with His will.

Before we explore the 15 Keys to Activating Your Ear to Hear the Voice of God, it is imperative that we first establish a biblical foundation. Understanding how God has historically spoken to His people provides the necessary framework for recognizing His voice in our personal lives today.

The Nature of God's Voice

God's Voice in Creation

The Scriptures begin with a profound declaration of divine authority: *"And God said, 'Let there be light,' and there was light"* (Genesis 1:3). Here, we witness the voice of God as the source of all existence, the force by which chaos is subdued, and order is established. This passage underscores that when God speaks, transformation is inevitable. His voice is not merely expressive; it is creative, life-giving, and sovereign.

The Still Small Voice

In 1 Kings 19:11-13, Elijah, a prophet accustomed to dramatic manifestations of God's power, encounters Him in an unexpected way—a "gentle whisper" or "still small voice." This account teaches us that God's voice is not always found in the earthquake, wind, or fire but often in the quiet, intimate moments of stillness. *True spiritual sensitivity requires the discipline of silence and the posture of attentiveness.*

The Voice of the Prophets

Throughout the Old Testament, God raised prophets as His spokesmen. Men like Isaiah, Jeremiah, and Ezekiel did not speak on their authority but were compelled by divine revelation. When God speaks through His prophets, His voice demands both obedience and reverence. *To hear God clearly, we must cultivate a prophetic awareness—one that recognizes His voice through His chosen vessels.*

Understanding God's Voice

The Role of the Holy Spirit

Jesus promised that the Holy Spirit would be our divine teacher and guide: *"When the Spirit of truth comes, he will guide you into all truth... and He will declare to you the things that are to come"* (John 16:13).

The Holy Spirit is not an optional add-on to our faith—He is the essential interpreter of God's voice in our lives. Without Him, spiritual deafness is inevitable.

Scripture as God's Voice

The Bible is not just a historical record; it is God-breathed (2 Timothy 3:16). Every word carries divine intent, making scripture the primary and most reliable means of hearing God's voice. *To neglect the Word is to neglect the voice of God.*

Prayer and Meditation

Jesus modeled a life of constant communion with the Father, often retreating to solitary places to pray (Luke 5:16). Prayer is not a one-sided monologue but an exchange, a place where we speak and listen. Meditation on His Word deepens our spiritual acuity, making His voice recognizable and distinguishable from the noise of the world.

Responding to God's Voice

Obedience and Action

Hearing God's voice requires more than recognition—it demands response. James 1:22 admonishes us, *"Be doers of the word, and not hearers only, deceiving yourselves."* Biblical figures such as Abraham, Moses, and Mary exemplified radical obedience. *Delayed obedience is disobedience.* When God speaks, our response must be immediate and wholehearted.

Discernment and Testing

Not every voice that claims to be divine originates from God. The apostle John warns, *"Beloved, do not believe every spirit, but test the spirits to see whether they are from God"* (1 John 4:1). Spiritual discernment is essential for distinguishing the voice of God from deception, emotions, and external influences.

Community and Accountability

God often confirms His voice through godly counsel and spiritual community. Proverbs 11:14 reminds us, *"In the multitude of counselors, there is safety."* Surrounding ourselves with mature believers provides a safeguard against misinterpretation and ensures that we remain aligned with biblical truth.

This introduction lays the groundwork for activating your ear to hear the voice of God. As we journey through the 15 Keys, expect a transformation in how you listen, respond, and walk in divine clarity. God is speaking—are you truly listening?

Ready, Set, Activate!

Key 1: Prayer

Prayer is one of the primary ways God speaks to His children. However, we live in a time where the power, sacredness, and intimacy of prayer are often overlooked. Many believers have abandoned the pursuit of God's voice and no longer value the discipline of prayer. Yet, prayer is essential—it awakens and activates our spiritual ears.

Throughout scripture, we see God responding and speaking clearly to those who seek Him in prayer. One of the reasons many believers struggle to recognize God's voice is that they have neglected prayer or were never truly acquainted with it. The old saying remains true: "Little prayer, little power; much prayer, much power." Our spiritual strength is directly tied to our prayer life. Without it, we risk becoming a generation of powerless Christians, believing that shouting and dancing alone will bring the supernatural move of God. But behind every great spiritual encounter is a foundation of prayer!

If you desire divine instructions for your life and destiny, you must establish a personal prayer life. No one else can do it for you—not your mother, not your pastor, and not your prayer partner. Prayer is simply communication with God, and communication is a two-way exchange. It's not just about speaking to Him; it's about listening as well.

Interestingly, Jesus never explicitly taught His disciples how to preach, prophesy, or even lay hands, but He did teach them how to pray. This reveals how much emphasis Jesus placed on prayer. Scripture commands us to *"pray without ceasing"* (1 Thessalonians 5:17). This doesn't mean we must pray 24/7, but rather, we should live in a posture of prayer—always in tune with God, always seeking His voice, and always making room for Him to speak.

Turn the Key Exercise

1. **Establish a Prayer Routine**: Choose a specific time each day to spend in prayer. Start with at least 5–10 minutes, and be consistent.

2. **Be Still and Listen**: After praying, take 2–5 minutes to sit in silence, allowing God to speak to your heart. Write down any thoughts, scriptures, or impressions you receive.

3. **Pray the Word**: Find a scripture about prayer (e.g., Philippians 4:6, Jeremiah 33:3) and incorporate it into your prayer time.

4. **Intercede for Others**: Each day, choose one person to pray for intentionally. Send them a message of encouragement or let them know you are praying for them.

Simple Prayer

"Father, I desire to know You more through prayer. Teach me to seek You with a sincere heart and to listen for Your voice. Help me to make prayer a daily priority and to remain in constant communion with You. Strengthen my spirit so that I may walk in power and authority. In Jesus' name, Amen."

Key 2: Posture – The Position of Alignment

Definition & Importance

Posture is defined as a particular way of dealing with or considering something—an approach or attitude. As believers, our posture is not just physical; it is the alignment of our hearts, minds, and spirits with God's will. Our posture determines how we receive from God and what He entrusts us with.

Just as an expectant mother must assume the correct posture to give birth, we must position ourselves correctly to receive the promises and purposes of God. When we are out of alignment—spiritually, emotionally, or mentally—it can hinder our ability to hear God's voice, receive revelation, and walk in divine purpose.

Spiritual Postures That Invite God's Presence

1. **A Posture of Humility**: *James 4:10* says, "Humble yourselves before the Lord, and He will lift you up." A heart filled with pride resists God's instruction, but humility makes room for His presence and guidance.

2. **A Posture of Obedience**: Many breakthroughs in scripture required a shift in posture. Naaman had to dip in the Jordan River (2 Kings 5), Moses had to remove his sandals (Exodus 3), and Peter had to step out of the boat (Matthew 14). Obedience positions us for divine encounters.

3. **A Posture of Expectancy**: Jesus often said, "According to your faith be it unto you" (Matthew 9:29). Expectancy is a posture of faith, believing that God is moving, even when we do not see it yet.

4. **A Posture of Surrender**: *Romans 12:1* urges us to present our bodies as living sacrifices. When we surrender, we allow God to shape our steps, timing, and direction.

5. **A Posture of Worship**: Worship is a physical and spiritual posture that shifts atmospheres. In 2 Chronicles 20, King Jehoshaphat and the people of Judah worshiped God, and He fought their battle for them.

Signs of a Wrong Posture

If you feel distant from God, check your posture. Ask yourself:

- **Has something infiltrated my heart?** Bitterness, offense, or unconfessed sin can block our spiritual receptivity.

- **Has my language shifted?** What we speak is a reflection of our posture. Complaining, doubt, and negativity signal misalignment.

- **Am I resistant to correction?** A teachable spirit is key to maintaining a posture that invites God's presence.

- **Am I positioned for birthing?** Just as a woman in labor must assume the right position, we must be in alignment to birth what God has placed in us.

Turn the Key: A Posture Check

Take time today to reflect on your spiritual posture. Sit in a quiet place and ask the Holy Spirit:

- Where am I out of alignment?
- What adjustments do I need to make?
- How can I reposition myself to hear You more clearly?

Write down any impressions, scriptures, or thoughts that come to mind, and commit to making the necessary shifts.

Prayer for Posture Alignment

Father, I come before You with a desire to be in the right posture before You. I repent for any area where I have moved out of alignment with Your will. Examine my heart, my thoughts, and my actions. Show me where I need to shift so that I can fully receive from You. I surrender my plans, my expectations, and my timeline. Help me to walk in humility, obedience, and faith. Position me for purpose, and let my posture invite Your presence into every area of my life. In Jesus' name, Amen.

Key 3: Pursuit – The Passionate Chase after God

Definition & Importance

Pursuit is an intentional and active chase after something of value. When we first encounter God, there is often a burning zeal to know Him, a deep longing to please Him, and an insatiable hunger to be in His presence. However, as time passes—just like in any relationship—familiarity can breed complacency. We may begin to take God's presence for granted, and our pursuit of Him can slowly diminish.

But here's the truth: The ability to hear from God, receive His guidance, and walk in His promises is directly tied to our pursuit of Him. God does not force Himself upon us; He reveals Himself to those who seek Him diligently.

Pursuit Is a Requirement, Not an Option

The Bible clearly states:

- "He is a rewarder of those who diligently seek Him." (*Hebrews 11:6*)
- "You will seek me and find me when you seek me with all your heart." (*Jeremiah 29:13*)
- "Seek the Lord while He may be found; call on Him while He is near." (*Isaiah 55:6*)

God's presence is not something we stumble upon—it is something we chase after. The depth of our relationship with Him depends on the intentionality of our pursuit.

Are You a Seeker?

The question today is not if God is speaking, but rather, are you seeking Him?

The reward of hearing His voice, receiving His power, and walking in purpose is on the **other side of your pursuit**.

Biblical Example: The Woman with the Issue of Blood

In *Mark 5:25-34*, we see a powerful example of relentless pursuit.

The woman with the issue of blood had suffered for twelve years with no relief. Yet, she decided nothing would stop her from getting to Jesus. Despite the crowds, despite the obstacles, despite her weakness, she pressed forward and touched the hem of His garment.

Her pursuit was met with instant healing.

What if she had given up? What if she had been content with watching Jesus from afar? She would have never received her miracle!

Likewise, your pursuit will determine your breakthrough. What are you willing to press past in order to reach Him?

What Can Hinder Your Pursuit?

If you feel distant from God, evaluate whether any of these factors are slowing your pursuit:

- **Distractions**: Are you too busy for God? Have the cares of life taken priority over your time with Him?
- **Complacency**: Are you spiritually "full" from yesterday's encounter and no longer hungry for more?
- **Doubt & Unbelief**: Do you struggle to believe that seeking God will actually produce results?
- **Sin & Compromise**: Is there anything in your life pulling you away from the presence of God?

Turn the Key: Rekindle Your Pursuit

1. **Carve out dedicated time daily**: Set a specific time each day to seek God through prayer, worship, and His Word.
2. **Remove distractions**: Identify things that steal your attention from God and create boundaries.
3. **Fast & Consecrate**: Fasting sharpens your spiritual hunger and refocuses your pursuit toward God.
4. **Engage in intentional worship**: Worship shifts the atmosphere and draws His presence near.

5. **Seek Him with expectancy**: Approach God with faith, believing that your pursuit will be met with His presence.

Prayer for a Renewed Pursuit

Father, reignite the fire within me to seek You passionately. I repent for allowing complacency, distractions, and weariness to slow my pursuit. I want to know You more, hear Your voice clearly, and walk in divine alignment. Teach me how to chase after You with all my heart, soul, and mind. Let my pursuit be relentless, just like the woman who pressed through the crowd to touch You. I declare that I am a seeker, and I will diligently pursue You every day of my life. In Jesus' name, Amen.

Key 4: Purge – A Cleansing for Clarity

Definition & Importance

To purge means to cleanse, remove impurities, or empty out what is unnecessary. It is an intentional process of removing anything that hinders our spiritual growth, clarity, and connection with God. Though purging is often uncomfortable, it is necessary for a deeper relationship with Him.

David understood this when he cried out:

"Purge me with hyssop, and I shall be clean; wash me, and I shall be whiter than snow." (*Psalm 51:7*)

This cry for cleansing came after he had sinned and realized he could not effectively serve or hear from God unless his life was purified. Likewise, there are seasons where God must purge us—spiritually, emotionally, and mentally—so that we can receive from Him clearly.

Why Do We Need to Be Purged?

Many times, we accumulate **spiritual clutter**—things that do not belong in our lives and that hinder our ability to hear from God. These can include:

- **Sin & Compromise**: Anything that contradicts God's Word dulls our spiritual ears.

- **Negative Influences**: The company we keep, the media we consume, and the conversations we entertain can cloud our discernment.

- **Unforgiveness & Bitterness**: Holding on to offense contaminates our hearts and blocks our spiritual growth.

- **Fear & Doubt**: When we allow fear to take root, it stifles our faith and restricts God's movement in our lives.

- **Old Mindsets & Habits**: Some ways of thinking, speaking, and acting must be removed for us to step into new levels of purpose.

The Ear Gate: Guarding Your Spiritual Intake

Our ears are one of the primary entry points to our spirit. What we hear has the power to influence our thoughts, emotions, and spiritual perception. If we are listening to negativity, gossip, or ungodly influences, it can distort how we hear God's voice.

This is why spiritual ear purging is necessary. Sometimes, God has to cleanse our hearing so that we can accurately receive divine instructions, warnings, and revelations.

Jesus said:

"He who has ears to hear, let him hear!" (*Matthew 11:15*)

If you feel like God's voice has become distant, it may be time for a purging of what you've been listening to.

Biblical Example: Isaiah's Purging Experience

In *Isaiah 6:5-7*, the prophet Isaiah had an encounter with God where he realized his unclean state:

"Woe is me! For I am undone; because I am a man of unclean lips... for my eyes have seen the King, the Lord of hosts!"

A seraphim then touched his lips with a burning coal and said:

"Behold, this has touched your lips; your iniquity is taken away, and your sin is purged."

This divine purging was necessary for Isaiah to move into greater prophetic clarity and purpose. Likewise, before we can walk into new assignments, God must refine and cleanse us.

The Benefits of Purging

Although purging is not comfortable, it produces:

- **Deliverance**: Freedom from sin, bondage, and anything restricting spiritual growth.
- **Divine Revelation**: A deeper understanding of God's will and purpose.
- **Supernatural Freedom**: A release from spiritual weights that were holding you back.
- **A Personal Revival**: A fresh fire in your spirit that renews passion for God.

Turn the Key: A Self-Purging Inventory

Ask yourself:

- Is there anything in my life that is contaminating my spirit?
- What am I listening to that might be dulling my ability to hear God?
- Are there relationships or habits that need to be removed?
- Am I truly ready for God to remove whatever is hindering me?

Write down anything that the Holy Spirit reveals, then surrender it to God in prayer.

Prayer for Purging & Cleansing

Father, I come before You asking for a divine purging in my life. Remove anything that is hindering my ability to hear from You, follow You, or walk fully in my purpose. Cleanse my heart, my mind, and my ears from anything that does not align with Your will. Purify my thoughts and remove every weight of sin, fear, or distraction. I surrender completely and ask that You fill me with Your Spirit, restoring my clarity, passion, and hunger for You. In Jesus' name, Amen.

Key 5: Pattern – Aligning Your Life for Growth

Definition & Importance

Patterns shape our lives. While we often blame our circumstances on external factors, the truth is that our repeated actions and habits determine our direction. Our minds are governed by the patterns we allow, and these patterns influence our ability to hear from God.

Jesus gave us a clear pattern to follow:

"But seek ye first the kingdom of God and His righteousness, and all these things shall be added unto you." (*Matthew 6:33*)

This is not a suggestion—it's a spiritual principle. When we establish a consistent pattern of seeking God first, we position ourselves for His presence, provision, and power.

The Power of Patterns

Patterns are created through:

- **Daily Routines**: What do you do first thing in the morning? How do you spend your time?
- **Habits & Hobbies**: Are they drawing you closer to God or distracting you?
- **Spiritual Disciplines**: Are you committed to prayer, fasting, and studying His Word?

Biblical Example: Job's Pattern of Worship

In *Job 1:5*, we see that Job had a daily pattern of presenting sacrifices to God. This consistent act of worship prepared him for the trials ahead. When adversity struck, his pattern kept him anchored in faith.

Turn the Key: Align Your Patterns

Take an honest inventory of your patterns:

- Are you prioritizing God daily?
- Do your routines reflect spiritual discipline?
- Are you making space to hear from Him consistently?

Challenge yourself: Recommit to the pattern of putting God first.

Prayer for Realignment

Father, help me establish patterns that honor You. Remove any habits that distract me from seeking You first. Teach me to be intentional about my routines so that I may live a life that is aligned with Your will. In Jesus' name, Amen.

Key 6: Pain – The Teacher of Transformation

Definition & Importance

Pain is a universal experience. It shapes, refines, and even redirects us. While no one desires pain, God often uses it as a tool to strengthen us. Some of the most painful moments in life can birth growth, faith, and a deeper relationship with God.

Biblical Example: Paul's Thorn in the Flesh

Paul cried out to God about his suffering: *"Three times I pleaded with the Lord to take it away from me. But He said to me, 'My grace is sufficient for you, for my power is made perfect in weakness.'"* (*2 Corinthians 12:8-9*)

God didn't remove Paul's pain—He used it to reveal His grace.

Pain Produces Purpose

- **Pain pushes us into God's presence.** We seek Him more fervently when we are hurting.
- **Pain builds spiritual maturity.** It stretches our faith and deepens our trust in God.
- **Pain unlocks new levels of grace.** When we endure suffering, God's grace becomes evident in our lives.

Turn the Key: Learn from Your Pain

Ask yourself:

- What is this pain teaching me?
- How is God using this situation for my growth?
- Am I allowing my pain to draw me toward God or push me away from Him?

Remember: Pain gives birth to grace. Embrace your grace place. Some of my greatest breakthroughs came through a painful situation. Pain validates and intensifies the oil on our lives! Don't give up, press through the pain. You're birthing something MAJOR!

Prayer for Strength in Pain

Father, I trust that my pain has a purpose. Even when I don't understand, I choose to believe that You are working all things for my good. Strengthen me and help me to rely on Your grace in every trial. In Jesus' name, Amen.

Key 7: Passion – Rekindling Your Fire for God

Definition & Importance

Passion fuels action. When we are passionate about something, we invest in it, we talk about it, and we make it a priority.

Ask yourself: Have you lost your passion for God?

We show passion for sports, careers, and relationships, but what about our relationship with Jesus?

What Passion for God Looks Like

- An excitement to seek Him daily
- A hunger for His presence and Word
- A willingness to serve Him wholeheartedly

Biblical Example: The Early Church's Passion

In *Acts 2:42-47*, the early believers were **devoted** to prayer, worship, and fellowship. Their passion caused the church to **grow rapidly** and sparked a revival.

Turn the Key: Reignite Your Passion

- Make time for personal worship
- Study the Word with fresh eyes
- Surround yourself with passionate believers

Prayer for Renewed Passion

Lord, reignite my passion for You. Remove any distractions that have caused my fire to dim. I long to seek You with my whole heart. Restore my excitement for Your presence. In Jesus' name, Amen.

Key 8: Perception – Seeing as God Sees

Teaching

Perception is the lens through which we interpret the world around us. It is shaped by our experiences, our exposure, and the environment we have been immersed in. While these factors help us navigate life, they can also act as blinders, preventing us from seeing and hearing God clearly.

Our upbringing, past wounds, religious traditions, and even societal norms can create filters that distort what God is revealing. If we have been conditioned to see life through fear, rejection, or human logic, we may miss divine instructions, seeing impossibilities where God is declaring victory.

The Bible warns us about this danger:

"You will indeed hear but never understand, and you will indeed see but never perceive. For this people's heart has grown dull, and with their ears they can barely hear, and their eyes they have closed..." (Matthew 13:14-15 ESV).

Jesus addressed the Pharisees repeatedly about this issue, not because they lacked knowledge, but because their exposure to religious tradition had blinded them to God's movement in the present. They were so rooted in their past understanding of God that they couldn't recognize the Messiah standing in front of them.

Likewise, our own experiences—whether personal pain, religious expectations, or cultural conditioning—can cloud our ability to perceive God's voice and direction. If we rely solely on what we know, we may resist what God is revealing. Our perception must be transformed by the Holy Spirit.

Realigning Our Perception with God's Vision

To clear our spiritual sight, we must intentionally seek God's perspective through His Word and prayer. Consider these scriptures:

- Romans 12:2 (NIV): *"Do not conform to the pattern of this world, but be transformed by the renewing of your mind. Then you will be able to test and approve what God's will is—his good, pleasing, and perfect will."*
    - Our transformation begins with renewing our minds so that we perceive God's will correctly.

- Isaiah 55:8-9 (NIV): *"For my thoughts are not your thoughts, neither are your ways my ways," declares the Lord. 'As the heavens are higher than the earth, so are my ways higher than your ways and my thoughts than your thoughts.'"*
    - God's perception is far beyond our own. We must seek His thoughts rather than lean on our limited experience.

- 2 Corinthians 4:18 (NIV): *"So we fix our eyes not on what is seen, but on what is unseen, since what is seen is temporary, but what is unseen is eternal."*

- o Our perception must shift from earthly limitations to eternal truth.

- Jeremiah 33:3 (NIV): *"Call to me and I will answer you and tell you great and unsearchable things you do not know."*

    - o When we seek God, He reveals hidden truths that go beyond our natural perception.

Turn the Key – Practical Exercise

1. **Identify Your Filters:** Take a moment to reflect on areas in your life where past experiences or exposure might be shaping your perception of God. Are you hesitant to trust because of past disappointments? Do you struggle to hear God's voice because of religious tradition or personal logic? Write these down.

2. **Renew Your Mind with Scripture:** Choose one of the verses above and meditate on it daily for the next week. Speak it aloud and ask God to reshape your perception through His truth.

3. **Practice Seeing Differently:** Spend time in prayer, asking God to reveal areas where your vision is clouded. Then, intentionally look at situations in your life through the lens of faith rather than fear or past experience.

4. **Listen without Bias:** The next time you pray or read scripture, ask the Holy Spirit to help you hear without the filter of your past. Write down any insights He gives you.

Prayer

Lord, open my eyes to see as You see. Remove any filters that distort my perception of You and Your will. Let my experiences and exposure never block me from hearing Your voice clearly. Renew my mind with Your Word and align my vision with Your truth. In Jesus' name, Amen.

Key 9: Persistence – Pressing In Until You Hear God

Teaching

Persistence is the key that unlocks breakthroughs in our spiritual lives. Many times, we assume that if we don't hear God immediately, He isn't speaking. But the truth is, God is always communicating—whether through His Word, our spirit, circumstances, or divine impressions. The problem is often not that God is silent, but that we give up too quickly in listening.

Jesus taught the importance of persistence in prayer:

"Then Jesus told his disciples a parable to show them that they should always pray and not give up." (Luke 18:1 NIV)

The enemy knows that if he can wear us down, distract us, or cause us to lose our persistence, we will miss what God is saying. There are multiple ways this can happen:

How Lack of Persistence Causes Us to Lose Out on Hearing God

1. **Failure to Persist in Prayer**

Prayer is our direct line to God. When we become inconsistent, our spiritual sensitivity dulls, and we struggle to recognize His voice.

- James 5:16 (NIV): *"The prayer of a righteous person is powerful and effective."*

- 1 Thessalonians 5:17 (NIV): *"Pray continually."*
- When we neglect prayer, we lose clarity, making it easier to be swayed by emotions, distractions, or worldly influences.

2. Neglecting Quiet Meditation

Many people pray but never take the time to listen for God's response. Constant noise—whether from social media, work, or entertainment—drowns out His voice.

- Psalm 46:10 (NIV): *"Be still, and know that I am God."*
- Isaiah 30:15 (NIV): *"In repentance and rest is your salvation, in quietness and trust is your strength."*
- If we do not persist in quieting our minds, we can become so distracted that we miss the whispers of the Holy Spirit.

3. Losing Social Consciousness of God's Presence

Being aware of God's presence in everyday life keeps us aligned with His will. When we lack persistence in acknowledging Him daily, we start making decisions based solely on human logic rather than divine guidance.

- Proverbs 3:5-6 (NIV): *"Trust in the Lord with all your heart and lean not on your own understanding; in all your ways submit to him, and he will make your paths straight."*

- John 10:27 (NIV): *"My sheep listen to my voice; I know them, and they follow me."*

- If we only seek God in crisis moments but neglect Him in our daily lives, we will struggle to recognize His voice when He speaks.

4. Failing to Persist in Fighting the Enemy

The enemy actively works to discourage, deceive, and distract us from hearing God. Spiritual warfare requires persistence because if we become passive, we give the devil an opportunity to distort God's voice or create confusion.

- Ephesians 6:12 (NIV): *"For our struggle is not against flesh and blood, but against the rulers, against the authorities, against the powers of this dark world and against the spiritual forces of evil in the heavenly realms."*

- Ephesians 6:18 (NIV): *"And pray in the spirit on all occasions with all kinds of prayers and requests. With this in mind, be alert and always keep on praying for all the Lord's people."*

- If we do not persist in resisting the devil (James 4:7), we will begin to hear his lies louder than God's truth.

Turn the Key – Practical Exercise

1. Set a Prayer Routine: Commit to a specific time daily to pray, even when you don't "feel" like it. Track your prayers and reflect on how God answers over time.

2. Practice Quiet Listening: After praying, take 5-10 minutes to sit in silence and invite God to speak. Write down any impressions, scriptures, instructions, or thoughts He places on your heart.

3. Acknowledge God Throughout the Day: Try pausing at random moments to say, "Lord, I recognize You here." This builds your awareness of His presence and welcomes the prophetic.

4. Engage in Spiritual Warfare: Memorize and declare scriptures that rebuke the enemy when doubts, distractions, or attacks arise.

Prayer

Father, give me the strength to persist in prayer, in stillness, in recognizing Your presence, and in spiritual warfare. I refuse to give up before I hear Your voice. Help me to push past distractions and discouragement so that I may walk in Your perfect will. In Jesus' name, Amen.

Key 10: Practice – Walking in Daily Obedience

Teaching

One of the most overlooked aspects of spiritual growth is practice—consistently acting on what God reveals to us. Many people assume that hearing from God requires a supernatural event, but often, He speaks through simple impressions, thoughts, and nudges in our spirit. The challenge is that we second-guess ourselves, hesitate, and sometimes outright disobey.

How many times have you heard people say, *"I should have followed my first mind"*? That first mind is often the Holy Spirit gently prompting us, yet doubt and fear cause us to override His leading. Instead of obeying immediately, we rationalize, overthink, or delay, missing divine opportunities.

The Bible tells us:

"Let this mind be in you which was also in Christ Jesus." (Philippians 2:5 NKJV)

This means we should train ourselves to think and act like Jesus—quick to obey, quick to move when God directs, and not enslaved to hesitation. Practicing obedience to the Holy Spirit is the key to walking in greater spiritual sensitivity. "Let" in this verse means to allow.

How to Practice Hearing and Obeying the Holy Spirit

1. **Obey Simple Instructions Quickly**

    - If a thought comes to mind to call someone, pray for them, or help a stranger, do it. Don't wait for a "sign"—the Holy Spirit often speaks through everyday thoughts.

    - John 10:27 (NIV): *"My sheep listen to my voice; I know them, and they follow me."*

    - Luke 11:28 (NIV): *"Blessed rather are those who hear the word of God and obey it."*

2. **Stop Second-Guessing Yourself**

    - Doubt is the enemy of obedience. Many times, we talk ourselves out of God's leading because we overanalyze.

    - James 1:22-23 (NIV): *"Do not merely listen to the word, and so deceive yourselves. Do what it says."*

    - Instead of hesitating, ask yourself: Does *God want me to do this?* If the answer is yes, act!

3. **Be Bold in Small Steps of Faith**

    - Obedience starts with small steps. When God places an idea or instruction in your mind, act on it without delay.

    - Example: If the Holy Spirit nudges you to apologize to someone, don't overthink it—just do it.

- 2 Corinthians 10:5 (NIV): *"We take captive every thought to make it obedient to Christ."*

4. **Trust that God is Teaching You**

    - Even if you're unsure whether a thought is from God, stepping out in faith allows you to grow in discernment.

    - Hebrews 5:14 (NIV): *"But solid food is for the mature, who by constant use have trained themselves to distinguish good from evil."*

    - The more you obey, the clearer His voice becomes.

Turn the Key – Practical Exercise

1. **Write Down Your First Thoughts.** Each morning, pray, then write down any thoughts, names, or ideas that come to mind. Throughout the day, act on them.

2. **Reflect on Missed Opportunities.** Journal moments when you second-guessed yourself and later realized it was God speaking. Learn from them.

3. **Commit to Immediate Obedience.** When a thought to do good arises, move quickly before doubt creeps in.

Simple Prayer

Holy Spirit, train my mind to be in sync with Yours. Help me to obey without hesitation, to trust that You are speaking, and to silence the doubts that cause me to second-guess. Let me practice hearing and obeying You daily, so I can walk in Your perfect will. In Jesus' name, Amen.

Key 11: Pace – Walking in Step with God's Timing

Teaching

Life moves fast, and society pressures us to move even faster. We rush to achieve success, hurry to prove ourselves, and anxiously push forward as if we're in competition with others. But moving at the wrong pace can lead to burnout, missed opportunities, and misalignment with God's will.

God has a divine pace for our lives—one that aligns with His purpose and prophetic timing. The enemy wants to push us into hasty decisions, unnecessary stress, and impatience, but God calls us to move in step with Him, not ahead of Him.

The Bible warns against rushing:

"There is a way that seems right to a man, but its end is the way of death." (Proverbs 14:12 NKJV)

When we rush ahead of God, we can force doors that weren't meant for us, enter seasons prematurely, or miss vital preparation. But when we walk at God's pace, we arrive at the right place at the right time, fully prepared for what He has ordained.

The Dangers of Rushing Through Life

1. **Rushing Leads to Burnout & Frustration**

- Trying to make things happen in our own strength leaves us exhausted and discouraged.
- Isaiah 40:31 (NIV): *"But those who hope in the Lord will renew their strength. They will soar on wings like eagles; they will run and not grow weary, they will walk and not be faint."*

2. **Rushing Causes Us to Miss Divine Appointments**

- When we move too fast, we overlook God's lessons, relationships, and divine setups.
- Ecclesiastes 3:1 (NIV): *"There is a time for everything, and a season for every activity under the heavens."*

3. **Rushing Can Lead to Wrong Decisions**

- Acting out of impatience rather than faith leads to mistakes.
- Example: Abraham and Sarah rushed God's promise, leading to unnecessary conflict (Genesis 16).
- Proverbs 19:2 (NIV): *"Desire without knowledge is not good—how much more will hasty feet miss the way!"*

God is Not Bound by Time

God operates outside of time. If He needs to accelerate us, He knows how to do it!

- **Jonah's Acceleration:** Jonah ran from God, but when the time came, God moved him quickly—in the belly of a fish! (Jonah 1:17).

- **Philip's Divine Transportation:** In Acts 8:39-40, the Spirit of the Lord suddenly moved Philip to another location after ministering.

- **Joseph's Overnight Promotion:** After years in prison, Joseph was elevated to the second most powerful man in Egypt in a single day (Genesis 41:14, 39-41).

When the time is right, God will move you supernaturally, without you having to force it!

Turn the Key – Practical Exercise

1. **Evaluate Your Current Pace:** Are you rushing ahead, or are you walking in sync with God? Write down areas where you feel impatient or pressured.

2. **Surrender Your Timeline:** Pray and release your personal deadlines to God, trusting His perfect plan.

3. **Move with Purpose, Not Pressure**: Ask God for wisdom before making big decisions—don't be pushed by external pressure.

Simple Prayer

Father, help me to walk at Your pace, not my own. Remove the spirit of hurry and anxiety from my heart. I trust Your divine timing and know that You will get me where I need to be at the right moment. Align my pace with my purpose, and let me move in sync with You. In Jesus' name, Amen.

Key 12: Praise – Unlocking the Power of Worship

Definition & Importance

Praise is more than just a song or a moment of celebration—it is a spiritual weapon, an act of faith, and a key to accessing God's presence.

Psalm 100:4 (NIV):

"Enter His gates with thanksgiving and His courts with praise; give thanks to Him and praise His name."

Praise is the posture of gratitude and victory. It shifts atmospheres, changes perspectives, and aligns us with heaven.

Why Praise is Powerful

- **It Invites God's Presence**: *"God inhabits the praises of His people" (Psalm 22:3).*
- **It Shifts Our Focus**: Praise moves our eyes from our problems to our Provider.
- **It Releases Breakthrough**: Paul and Silas praised in prison, and their chains fell off (Acts 16:25-26).

Biblical Example: Jehoshaphat's Battle (2 Chronicles 20:21-22)

When King Jehoshaphat faced an overwhelming enemy, he put worshippers at the front of the battle. As they praised, God fought for them.

Turn the Key: Activate Your Praise

- Praise before the breakthrough, not just after.
- Make praise a daily discipline, not just an emotional response.

Prayer for a Life of Praise

Father, I choose to praise You in every season. I lift my voice in worship, knowing that You are faithful. Let my praise shift atmospheres, break chains, and bring Your presence into my life. In Jesus' name, Amen.

Key 13: Pivoting – Embracing God's Divine Redirection

Definition & Importance

A pivot is a shift in direction without losing balance. Spiritually, pivoting means embracing God's redirection without resisting His plan.

Proverbs 3:5-6 (NIV):

"Trust in the Lord with all your heart and lean not on your own understanding; in all your ways submit to Him, and He will make your paths straight."

Life doesn't always go as planned, but God's purpose is never interrupted—only redirected.

When Does God Call Us to Pivot?

- **When Our Plans Don't Align With His**: Sometimes, we must let go of our agenda.
- **When Doors Close**: Closed doors are often divine protection or preparation.
- **When He's Preparing Us for Greater**: Sometimes, God pivots us into a season of growth before the next assignment.

Biblical Example: Paul's Divine Pivot (Acts 16:6-10)

Paul wanted to go to Asia, but the Holy Spirit redirected him to Macedonia. That pivot led to a major revival in Europe.

Turn the Key: Trust the Pivot

- Let go of **what's familiar** to embrace **what's divine.**

- Ask: **Is this a delay or a redirection?**

- **Follow peace**—God's pivots come with **confirmation and clarity.**

Prayer for Trust in God's Direction

Lord, I surrender my plans and trust Your direction. When You pivot me, help me to move without fear. Align my steps with Your purpose, and give me peace in the process. In Jesus' name, Amen.

Key 14: Proclaiming – Declaring the Word with Boldness

Definition & Importance

To proclaim is to declare truth boldly. Our words shape our reality, and when we proclaim God's promises, we align with His will.

Proverbs 18:21 (NIV):

"The tongue has the power of life and death, and those who love it will eat its fruit."

What are you speaking over your life? Faith-filled proclamations invite heaven to move.

Why Proclaiming God's Word Is Essential

- **It Increases Faith**: Speaking God's Word reinforces belief.
- **It Shifts Circumstances**: Jesus spoke to the storm, and it obeyed (*Mark 4:39*).
- **It Releases Power**: Life and death are in the power of the tongue (*Proverbs 18:21*).

Biblical Example: Ezekiel and the Dry Bones (Ezekiel 37:1-10)

God told Ezekiel to prophesy to the dry bones. As he spoke, life was restored.

Turn the Key: Speak Life

- Stop speaking doubt and start declaring destiny.
- Speak scripture over your situation daily.

Prayer for Bold Proclamation

Lord, let my words align with Your truth. Teach me to proclaim life, victory, and faith over every area of my life. May my declarations shift my atmosphere and invite Your will to be done. In Jesus' name, Amen.

Key 15: Pleasing God – Living for an Audience of One

Definition & Importance

Many people live for the approval of others, but true fulfillment comes from pleasing God alone.

Galatians 1:10 (NIV):

"Am I now trying to win the approval of human beings, or of God? If I were still trying to please people, I would not be a servant of Christ."

Living to please God leads to peace, purpose, and eternal reward.

What Pleases God?

- **Faith**: *"Without faith, it is impossible to please God"* (Hebrews 11:6).
- **Obedience**: *"If you love Me, keep My commandments"* (John 14:15).
- **Holiness**: *"Be holy, because I am holy"* (1 Peter 1:16).

Biblical Example: Enoch's Walk with God (Genesis 5:24)

Enoch pleased God so much that he was taken without experiencing death.

Turn the Key: Live for God's Approval

- Seek His will, not public validation.

- Choose obedience over popularity.
- Let your actions reflect faith, not fear.

Prayer for a Life that Pleases God

Father, I choose to live for You alone. Remove any desire for human approval and help me to walk in faith, obedience, and holiness. Let my life be pleasing in Your sight. In Jesus' name, Amen.

Conclusion: Unlocking a Life of Hearing God

Throughout this journey, we have explored **the keys to developing** an ear to hear God. Each key—whether it was posture, pursuit, purging, persistence, or praise—has been a stepping stone toward greater spiritual clarity and deeper intimacy with the Father.

But the journey does not stop here.

Hearing from God is not a one-time event—it is a lifelong relationship. Just like any meaningful connection, it requires intentionality, consistency, and a heart that remains open to His voice.

The Responsibility of Hearing

God is always speaking, but the real question is: Are we truly listening?

Hearing God is not just about receiving direction for our personal lives; it is about aligning our hearts with His will so that we can be used as prophetic vessels for His Kingdom. When we fine-tune our spiritual ears, we position ourselves to be:

- **Led by His Spirit**: No longer walking in confusion but in divine clarity.
- **Anchored in Truth**: Not swayed by emotions or the world's opinions.
- **Empowered for Purpose**: Equipped to fulfill the assignments He has placed before us.

Staying in Position to Hear

As you close this devotional, let these truths remain foundational in your walk with God:

1. **Keep seeking**: Never grow complacent. The more you seek Him, the clearer His voice becomes (*Jeremiah 29:13*).

2. **Guard your spiritual ears**: Be mindful of what you allow into your heart and mind (*Proverbs 4:23*).

3. **Embrace the process**: Hearing God often requires waiting, trust, and surrender (*Ecclesiastes 3:11*).

4. **Walk in faith**: Even when you don't understand, trust that His voice will always lead you right (*Hebrews 11:6*).

Your Next Step

Now that you have received these keys, the question remains: What will you do with them?

God is calling you to apply what you have learned. To actively align your posture, pursue Him diligently, embrace the necessary pruning, and persist in seeking His presence. The reward of hearing Him is a life transformed, a heart at peace, and a destiny fulfilled.

Are you ready to unlock the next level of your spiritual hearing?

Then step forward in faith. Listen closely. He is speaking.

Final Prayer

Father, thank You for taking me on this journey of learning to hear Your voice. I surrender my ears, my heart, and my mind to You. Help me to remain in position, to stay in pursuit, and to trust Your leading every step of the way. Let my life be a reflection of Your voice, and may I always walk in obedience to Your will. In Jesus' name, Amen.

You now hold the keys. Use them well. 🔑🔥

Biblical Meditations to Help Hear from God

Meditating on God's Word is a powerful way to tune your spiritual ears and become more sensitive to His voice. Below is a list of biblical meditations that will help you develop the ability to hear from God clearly.

1. Seeking God's Voice

☐ Jeremiah 33:3: *"Call to me and I will answer you and tell you great and unsearchable things you do not know."* Meditation: God desires to speak to you. Take time to sit in silence and listen for His whisper.

☐ John 10:27: *"My sheep listen to my voice; I know them, and they follow me."* Meditation: As a believer, you belong to God. Trust that you have the ability to recognize His voice.

☐ Psalm 46:10: *"Be still, and know that I am God."* Meditation: Silence the noise of the world and sit quietly in God's presence, allowing Him to speak.

2. Removing Spiritual Blockages

☐ Psalm 51:10: *"Create in me a clean heart, O God, and renew a right spirit within me."* Meditation: Ask God to purge anything hindering your ability to hear Him—sin, distractions, or doubt.

☐ Hebrews 12:1: *"Let us throw off everything that hinders and the sin that so easily entangles. And let us run with perseverance the race marked out for us.* "Meditation: Reflect on anything weighing you down and surrender it to God so you can hear Him more clearly.

📖 Isaiah 59:2: *"But your iniquities have separated you from your God; your sins have hidden his face from you so that he will not hear."* Meditation: Repent of any known sin and ask for God's restoration and renewed sensitivity to His voice.

3. Trusting God's Timing

📖 Ecclesiastes 3:1: *"There is a time for everything and a season for every activity under the heavens.* "Meditation: God's timing is perfect. Trust that He will speak when the moment is right.

📖 Lamentations 3:25: *"The Lord is good to those who wait for him, to the soul who seeks him.* "Meditation: Patience is part of hearing from God. Wait on Him with expectation.

📖 Isaiah 40:31: *"But those who wait on the Lord shall renew their strength; they shall mount up with wings like eagles.* "Meditation: In waiting, God strengthens your faith. Listen for His whispers in the waiting.

4. Aligning Your Heart with God's Will

📖 Romans 12:2: *"Do not conform to the pattern of this world, but be transformed by the renewing of your mind. Then you will be able to test and approve what God's will is—his good, pleasing and perfect will."*

Meditation: Ask God to align your thoughts with His so that you can discern His voice.

📖 Matthew 6:33: *"But seek first the kingdom of God and his righteousness, and all these things will be given to you as well."*
Meditation: Put God first in every area of your life and listen for His direction.

📖 Proverbs 3:5-6: *"Trust in the Lord with all your heart and lean not on your own understanding; in all your ways submit to him, and he will make your paths straight.* "Meditation: Release control. Ask God to guide your steps as you listen for His leading.

5. *The Power of God's Word*

📖 Hebrews 4:12: *"For the word of God is alive and active. Sharper than any double-edged sword, it penetrates even to dividing soul and spirit."*
Meditation: God speaks through His Word—make scripture meditation a daily habit.

📖 Joshua 1:8: *"Keep this Book of the Law always on your lips; meditate on it day and night, so that you may be careful to do everything written in it. Then you will be prosperous and successful.* "Meditation: Biblical meditation brings clarity and success. Ask God to reveal His truth as you study His Word.

📖 Psalm 119:105: *"Your word is a lamp to my feet and a light to my path."*

Meditation: Let scripture guide your decisions. Listen for direction through the Word.

6. Asking and Expecting to Hear from God

📖 James 1:5: *"If any of you lacks wisdom, you should ask God, who gives generously to all without finding fault, and it will be given to you."* Meditation: Ask for wisdom and clarity, and trust that God will respond.

📖 Matthew 7:7-8: *"Ask and it will be given to you; seek and you will find; knock and the door will be opened to you."* Meditation: Consistent seeking leads to revelation. Keep asking, seeking, and knocking.

📖 Isaiah 30:21: *"Whether you turn to the right or to the left, your ears will hear a voice behind you, saying, 'This is the way; walk in it.'"* Meditation: God's voice will direct your path. Be still and listen for His instruction.

7. Walking in Obedience to What You Hear

📖 James 1:22: *"Do not merely listen to the word, and so deceive yourselves. Do what it says.* "Meditation: True hearing leads to action. Ask God for the strength to obey His voice.

📖 John 14:23: *"Anyone who loves me will obey my teaching. My Father will love them, and we will come to them and make our home with them."*

Meditation: Obedience invites God's presence. When you hear, be ready to act.

📖 1 Samuel 15:22: *"To obey is better than sacrifice, and to heed is better than the fat of rams."* Meditation: Obedience is key to continued revelation. Ask God to help you follow His voice wholeheartedly.

Final Thought: Position Yourself to Hear

God is always speaking, but we must be intentional about positioning ourselves to hear. Use these scriptures as a daily devotional guide to train your spiritual ears and grow in sensitivity to His voice.

www.ingramcontent.com/pod-product-compliance
Lightning Source LLC
Chambersburg PA
CBHW060034180426
43196CB00045B/2680